Scary States (of Mind)

Horror in Washington

by Rachel Rose

Consultant: Debbie Felton
Professor of Classics
University of Massachusetts
Amherst, Massachusetts

Bearport Publishing
Minneapolis, Minnesota

Credits

Cover, © Kim Jones, © Michal Balada/Shutterstock, © Tom Reichner/Shutterstock, © Tory Kallman/Shutterstock, © Marco Rolleman/Shutterstock, and © Nithid/Shutterstock; 3, Edmund Lowe Photography; 4-5, © Kim Jones, ©Dima Aslanian/Shutterstock, and ©Scott E Read/Shutterstock; 7 (inset), Granola/Wikimedia Commons/Creative Commons; 7, Benjamin Cody/Wikimedia Commons/Public Domain; 8, © Andrew Lam/Shutterstock; 9, © Andrey_Kuzmin/Shutterstock and © DarkBird/Shutterstock; 10, Wikimedia Commons/Public Domain; 11, © EchoGolf Photography/Shutterstock; 12L, © marilyn barbone/Shutterstock; 12R, © Zerbor/Shutterstock; 12-13, © shuttersv/Shutterstock and © Baba Mora/Shutterstock; 14, © Lario Tus/Shutterstock; 15, Courtesy Central Washington University; 16, © Dinga/Shutterstock, © Social Media Hub/Shutterstock, and © arda savasciogullari/Shutterstock; 17, © Rob Larsen; 18, Wikimedia Commons/Public Domain; 19, © Christopher Boswell/Shutterstock; 20, © Roman Sigaev/Shutterstock; 21, Courtesy Tahoma Public Library and © Halfpoint/Shutterstock; 23, © Matt Ragen/Shutterstock; and 24, © Stefan Nielsen/Shutterstock.

President: Jen Jenson
Director of Product Development: Spencer Brinker
Editor: Allison Juda
Designer: Micah Edel
Cover: Kim Jones

Library of Congress Cataloging-in-Publication Data

Names: Rose, Rachel, 1968- author.
Title: Horror in Washington / Rachel Rose.
Description: Minneapolis, Minnesota : Bearport Publishing Company, [2021] | Series: Scary states (of mind) | Includes bibliographical references and index.
Identifiers: LCCN 2020000521 (print) | LCCN 2020000522 (ebook) | ISBN 9781647470807 (library binding) | ISBN 9781647470906 (ebook)
Subjects: LCSH: Haunted places—Washington (State)—Juvenile literature. | Ghosts—Washington (State)—Juvenile literature. | Washington (State)—Miscellanea—Juvenile literature.
Classification: LCC BF1472.U6 R6653 2021 (print) | LCC BF1472.U6 (ebook) | DDC 133.109797—dc23
LC record available at https://lccn.loc.gov/2020000521
LC ebook record available at https://lccn.loc.gov/2020000522

For more information, write to Bearport Publishing, 5357 Penn Avenue South, Minneapolis MN 55419. Printed in the United States of America.

CONTENTS

Horror in Washington

Washington is famous for is its natural beauty. But did you know there is a darker, more **sinister** side to the Evergreen State? Beware the ghostly figures that rattle and **wail** and hide in the shadows.

Get ready to read four terrifying tales about Washington. Turn the page . . . if you dare.

Spirits Acting Out

Mount Baker Theatre, Bellingham

The Mount Baker Theatre in Bellingham first opened in 1927. Today, singers and actors aren't the only ones who appear at the theater.

A friendly **spirit** named Judy moves things around and calls out peoples' names. Some have seen her ghostly figure floating in hallways. Others have felt a chilling rush of cold air.

Mount Baker Theatre soon after it opened in 1927

Mount Baker Theatre today

Over 100 years ago, Judy lived in a **boarding house** in downtown Bellingham. She loved to sing and dance in nearby **saloons**. One evening, she fell ill and died in her room. Later, the boarding house was torn down to make room for the theater. Judy's room was located where the stage stands today. Even though she is dead, it seems that Judy still loves to perform.

In the 1930s, a black panther from a traveling circus died during a show. Today, its ghost has been seen prowling around the theater.

HAUNTED STREETS

Pike Place Market, Seattle

Shoppers can find fresh produce and handmade goods at Pike Place Market. They can also find a surprise at the market—a princess ghost!

Princess Angeline was the daughter of the famous Duwamish leader Chief Seattle. When their tribe was forced to move off their land in 1855, Princess Angeline refused to leave. Many say her spirit still hasn't left.

Princess Angeline

Pike Place Market

Each year, about 10 million people visit Pike Place Market. That's about 30,000 people every day!

The ghost of Angeline is often seen wandering around the market. She walks slowly and hunched over. The princess wears a red headscarf and a shawl. Some say they have seen her sitting on a blanket surrounded by baskets to sell. Angeline appears real until would-be buyers get closer. Then, she **vanishes** into thin air!

CENTER
COMEDY

Lola in Kamola

Central Washington University, Ellensburg

Lola was a student living in Kamola Hall at Central Washington University during World War II (1939–1945). Her sweetheart was killed in the war. Heartbroken, she hanged herself from the rafters in the attic of Kamola Hall. Some say she was wearing her wedding dress.

Kamola Hall around the time of World War II

Students report hearing footsteps coming from the empty attic at Kamola Hall. Some hear wailing. Others say doors open and close by themselves.

In 2002, a photographer came to take photos at the university. All of the pictures he took at Kamola Hall were ruined. Many were just black. Some showed a strange fog everywhere. There is even a ghostly figure in the background of one photograph. Could it be Lola looking for her lost love?

Kamola Hall today

Ghostly Bells

Old City Hall, Tacoma

Old City Hall is a well-known **landmark** in downtown Tacoma. It served as a government building for many years. There was a jail in its basement at one time. Later on, it housed a restaurant and offices. Today, most of the building sits quiet and empty. Or does it?

Old City Hall around 1919

The bell tower is
ten stories high.

There have been many reports of **eerie** activities in the building. The clock tower bells ring late at night when no one is there. Lights turn on and off. The elevator goes up and down by itself. Shadowy figures have been seen in the hallways.

People believe the ghost of a night watchman named Gus is responsible for many of the activities. Has he become a lonely **phantom** looking for attention?

Gus played pranks on the restaurant. Bottles fell over, and doors slammed shut by themselves. But Gus would stop when the workers spoke to him.

Inside Old City Hall

Spooky Spots in Washington

GLOSSARY

boarding house (BORD-ing HOUSS) a lodging house where rooms and meals are provided

eerie (IHR-ee) mysterious or strange

landmark (LAND-mark) a building or place that is easily seen and recognized

phantom (FAN-tuhm) a ghost or ghostlike image

saloons (suh-LOONZ) places where people can buy and drink alcohol

sinister (SIN-uh-stur) harmful or evil

spirit (SPIHR-it) a ghost

vanishes (VAN-ish-uhz) disappears from sight

wail (WAYL) to cry out in pain or sadness

INDEX

READ MORE

Camisa, Kathryn. *Ghostly Theaters (Tiptoe Into Scary Places).* New York: Bearport (2018).

Camisa, Kathryn. *Creepy Schools (Tiptoe Into Scary Places).* New York: Bearport (2018).

LEARN MORE ONLINE

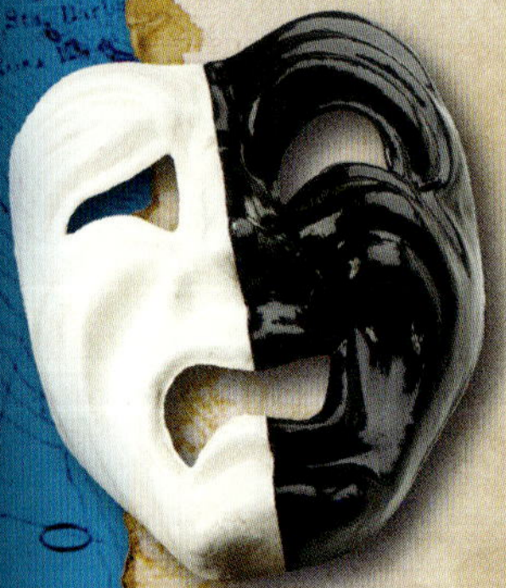

1. Go to **www.factsurfer.com**
2. Enter "**Horror in Washington**" into the search box.
3. Click on the cover of this book to see a list of websites.

ABOUT THE AUTHOR

Rachel Rose lives in San Francisco. She grew up in Ireland and loved listening to scary stories about banshees from her grandmother.